```
cousin(X,Y)  - parent(X,Xp) & parent(Y,Yp) & cousin(Xp,Yp).
```

We would like to compute the relation *closerCousins*, defined by $closerCousins(x, y, u, v)$ if and only if $cousin(x, y)$ and $cousin(u, v)$ and x and y are "closer related" than u and v in the obvious sense

closerCousins can be computed with a *temporal logic* [Kro87,McArt76,ReUr71] formula *cousin(x,y)* **before** *cousin(u,v)*, assuming appropriate temporal semantics In this paper, we formally define both syntax and semantics of temporal logic queries

To define semantics of temporal logic queries, we have to introduce a new Datalog semantics first Traditionally, there is no notion of time associated with Datalog programs all the cousins belong to the same "snapshot" of *cousin* relation Therefore, Datalog semantics is associated with the state of the database at the "fixpoint time." We call this semantics *static* because the intermediate states of the database are of no semantic interest, and only the (static) state at the fixpoint time is meaningful

In this paper, we adapt Datalog to describe an evolution of a database by introducing time Specifically, we assume that time instances are described by natural numbers with the present being time instance 0 [1] We can now define the evolution of a database in time Given D_i, the state of a database at some time instance $i \geq 0$, D_{i+1}, the state of the database at time instance $i + 1$, is obtained by applying all the program rules simultaneously to D_i This process results in an (infinite) sequence of database states $D_0, D_1, D_2, \ldots$ Clearly, there is no need to assume the existence of a fixpoint Since we assign meanings to the elements of this sequence, we refer to the interpretation of a Datalog program with this sequence as *dynamic* semantics We will use the term *dynamic Datalog* to refer to Datalog with dynamic semantics

As shown in [KeTu89], dynamic semantics of databases can be described with various formalisms, some of them unrelated to Datalog. In this paper we concentrate on using the following two types of Datalog programs. The first one will be *pure Datalog*, without negations The second will be *negated Datalog*, $\text{Datalog}^{\neg}$ (negations being allowed only in the bodies of rules) with *inflationary semantics* [AbVi88,GuSh86,KoPa88] We chose inflationary semantics as it can be applied to arbitrary negated Datalog programs

Once semantics for dynamic databases is defined, the next step is to define a query

[1] Of course, time can be "shifted," to describe finite past too

language about future time instances of dynamic databases One of the attractive features of Datalog is the unity of the data model and the query language Since we selected Datalog to describe dynamic databases we would like to use the standard query language on Datalog, i e *Datalog queries* that simply constitute intentional database predicates (IDB predicates) taken at "fixpoint time" Although Datalog queries determine the state of a database at the fixpoint time, one can still attempt to use them to provide answers about intermediate database states as well This might be achievable by expanding the underlying Datalog program so that it still "remembers" important intermediate states at the fixpoint time Alternatively, we can choose a future-related fragment of *predicate temporal logic* [Kro87,McArt76,ReUr71] as a query language for dynamic Datalog and its extensions

In this paper, we study the relationship between Datalog queries and temporal logic queries Clearly, any Datalog query $Q(\mathbf{x})$, where $\mathbf{x}$ is the vector of free variables in Q can be expressed in a temporal logic for Datalog or Datalog$^\neg$ program P as $\diamond Q(\mathbf{x})$, where $\diamond$ is the possibility operator of temporal logic [Kro87] Intuitively, $Q(\mathbf{x})$ is true at the "fixpoint time" if at *some* point in the execution of program P, $Q(\mathbf{x})$ becomes true (this latter statement is denoted by $\diamond Q(\mathbf{x})$) Thus, temporal logic is at least as powerful as Datalog queries Indeed, as we show, temporal logic queries have more expressive power than Datalog queries for both Datalog and Datalog$^\neg$ programs with inflationary semantics

It is technically challenging to analyze when Datalog queries are as powerful as temporal logic queries We will show that under mild restrictions, the *existential* fragment of temporal logic (to be defined later), has the same expressive power as Datalog queries for safe Datalog$^\neg$ with inflationary semantics Among other things, it follows from this that under some mild restrictions the existential fragment of temporal logic for Datalog$^\neg$ with inflationary semantics *collapses to a single possibility operator*, i e any temporal logic formula from the existential fragment can be expressed with a single possibility operator $\diamond$

It may be worthwhile to state succinctly the advantages of temporal logic queries over Datalog queries for dynamic semantics defined by Datalog programs and its extensions First, as claimed above, they have more expressive power for Datalog and Datalog$^\neg$ with inflationary semantics Second, they do not depend on existence of any fixpoints for some of Datalog extensions, e g for Datalog$^{\neg *}$ (the extension of Datalog$^{\neg}$ where negations are allowed both in the body and the head of a rule) [AbVi89][2] Third, we believe that temporal logic queries are conceptually simpler For the specific case of Datalog$^{\neg}$ with inflationary semantics, any Datalog query Q can be expressed as $\diamond Q$ in temporal logic, however, as we show later, it seems that some of the temporal logic queries expressible as Datalog queries, can be expressed so only in a very complicated way

We now describe the organization of the rest of the paper while highlighting our contributions. In Section 2, we define both some preliminary concepts that will be used in Section 4 and define a query language about dynamic databases whose syntax is based on temporal logic and whose semantics is based on dynamic Datalog and its extensions In Section 3, we describe related work In Section 4, we analyze the relative expressive powers of temporal logic and Datalog queries for Datalog and Datalog$^{\neg}$ programs with dynamic semantics We show how domain-independent[3] and domain-dependent queries from the existential fragment of temporal logic can be expressed with Datalog queries Our technique is based on expressing temporal queries with *ordering predicates* we introduce in the paper These predicates characterize the relative times when various tuples are inserted into the IDB predicates, and, most importantly, can be computed using safe Datalog$^{\neg}$ rules

2 Preliminaries

In this section, we define preliminary concepts that are necessary for understanding the material presented in Section 4 However, certain concepts, mainly in Section 2 2 constitute our original contribution We will delineate these concepts from the work of other researchers

2.1 Datalog and Its Extensions

A *pure Datalog program* is a finite set of Horn clauses, i e. rules of the form $A \leftarrow B_1 \wedge \ldots \wedge B_n$, where A is a positive literal and $B_1, \ldots, B_n$ are positive literals or built-in predicates $x_i = x_j$, $x_i \neq x_j$, $x_i > x_j$, etc (the x_i's are variables or constants). A *negated Datalog*

[2] Actually, as stated above, temporal logic queries can be applied to any formalism able to express dynamic semantics

[3] This concept corresponds to the familiar one for static databases and will be defined precisely later

program, Datalog$^{\neg}$ program, is a set of rules in which negations are allowed in the body of a rule Datalog program P has two types of predicates *Extensional database predicates (EDB predicates)* never appear in the head of a rule in P For each EDB predicate, P has a set of ground atoms (facts) associated with that predicate The predicates appearing in the left-hand side of some rule in P are called *intentional database predicates (IDB predicates)* For a general survey of Datalog, see e g [Ull88]

If P is a Datalog or Datalog$^{\neg}$ program, the *schema* of P, $sch(P)$, is the database schema consisting of schemas of all the relations occurring in P A *domain* of program P, DOM_P, is the domain associated with schema $sch(P)$ The domains can be infinite in general.

The semantics of Datalog programs is traditionally defined in terms of the least fixpoint, whereas there are several types of semantics proposed in the literature for Datalog$^{\neg}$ In this paper, we will use *inflationary semantics* [AbVi88,GuSh86 KoPa88] for Datalog$^{\neg}$ because it is applicable to all Datalog$^{\neg}$ programs Both types of semantics are defined with a mapping $EVAL$ from EDB and IDB predicates to IDB predicates of a program P, which, for a given instance of IDB predicates D, computes all the new facts derivable from D and from EDB predicates by applying rules in P [4] IDB predicates are initially made empty The least fixpoint semantics is defined as the fixpoint of the recurrence equation $D_{i+1} = EVAL(D_i)$, and inflationary semantics with the fixpoint of the recurrence equation $D_{i+1} = D_i \cup EVAL(D_i)$ (a fixpoint is reached when $D_i = D_{i+1}$) These two semantics coincide on pure Datalog programs We call these types of semantics, based on fixpoints *static* because they are defined only in terms of the "final" (static) result.

Another meaning of Datalog and Datalog$^{\neg}$ programs can be associated with the entire sequence of database states $D_0, D_1, D_2, \ldots, D_n,$ We call this kind of semantics *dynamic* because it defines the "dynamics" of Datalog and Datalog$^{\neg}$ programs This dynamic semantics will become important below when we define semantics of temporal logic

Next, we define safety Intuitively, a rule is *safe* if it cannot produce new constants Formally, we define *limited* variables as in [Ull88] A variable is limited if it either occurs positively in one of the predicates in the body of a rule or can be equated to a constant or to some other variable that occurs positively in the body of a rule through a chain of

[4] For precise definition of $EVAL$ see [Ull88, p 115]

equalities A Datalog$^\neg$ rule is called *safe* [AbVi88] if all the variables in the head of the rule are limited[5] A Datalog$^\neg$ program is *safe* if all of its rules are safe Clearly, safe Datalog$^\neg$ programs cannot introduce new symbols when rules are applied to a database Therefore a safe Datalog$^\neg$ program with inflationary semantics always has a fixpoint [AbVi88] The definition of safety presented here (and in [AbVi88]) differs from the conventional definition of safety from [Ull88] In [Ull88], a rule is safe if all the variables (not only in the head but also in the body of a rule) are limited Therefore, the conventional definition of safety [Ull88] is more restrictive than the definition from [AbVi88] adopted in this paper.

If program P is not safe then it generates *all* the new symbols from DOM_P because a variable in the head not occurring positively in the body is not bound to any value during the rule matching process and, therefore, is assigned any value from DOM_P. Consequently, we get infinite relations for unsafe programs. To avoid this situation. we consider *only* safe programs in this paper

A *Datalog query* for a Datalog or Datalog$^\neg$ program P is a predicate Q appearing among the IDB predicates of P.

2.2 Temporal Logic as a Query Language

In this section, we define a query language based on temporal logic The syntax of a query language is based on a predicate temporal logic and the semantics either on pure Datalog or on Datalog$^\neg$ Separately, temporal logic and Datalog have been extensively studied before. One of our contributions in this paper lies in *combining* the two separate concepts in one integral approach

We consider the standard predicate temporal logic [McArt76,ReUr71] with standard temporal operators $\diamond$ (*possibility*), $\square$ (*necessity*), $\circ$ (*next-moment*), binary operators **while**, **until**, **unless**, **before**, **atnext** [Kro87], and with time defined with natural numbers A **atnext** B is true if A is true at the first time B is true If B is never true then **atnext** yields false[6] Definitions of other operators can be found in [Krö87] [Krö87] also shows how all of them can be expressed in terms of **atnext**

[5] Actually, this definition of safety is a rewritten definition of *strong safety* from [AbVi88]

[6] Our **atnext** operator *differs* from the definition of **atnext** in [Kro87] Since each of the **atnext** operators can be expressed in terms of the other, the slight alteration of meaning does not affect our results

Semantics of a temporal logic formula is defined with a *temporal structure* [Kro87], which comprises the values of all its predicates at *all* the times in the future Formally, a temporal structure is a mapping $K \; N \rightarrow \mathcal{P}_1 \times \quad \times \mathcal{P}_k$, where N is a set of natural numbers, and $\mathcal{P}_i$ is the set of all the possible interpretations of a predicate P_i The mapping K assigns to each time instance (a natural number) the truth values for predicates P_i We will use K_t instead of $K(t)$ to denote the value of the temporal structure K at time t We make an important assumption, natural in the database context, that *domains of predicates do not change over time*

From the database perspective, a temporal structure can be viewed as an infinite sequence of database states, i e $D_0, D_1, D_2,$ Various methods for defining sequences of database states have been considered in [KeTu89] In this paper, we consider Datalog with dynamic semantics and Datalog$^\neg$ with dynamic inflationary semantics as two mechanisms for defining sequences of database states Specifically, a Datalog or Datalog$^\neg$ program P defines the temporal structure $K^P = D_0, D_1, D_2,$, where D_i is the state of the database (i e instances of predicates from $sch(P)$) at time i, such that $D_{i+1} = EVAL(D_i)$ for $i = 1, 2, 3,$, where $EVAL$ is the mapping discussed on page 5

Sequences of database states have been studied before in [GiTa86 KeTu89,Via87] Also, [SeSh87] defines time sequences and operations on them This research is related to our work because temporal structures can be defined with these sequences However, in this paper, we concentrate on the sequences defined with Datalog and Datalog$^\neg$ programs and use them to define semantics of temporal logic queries.

A temporal logic formula ϕ on Datalog or Datalog$^\neg$ program P, with all the predicates in ϕ belonging to schema $sch(P)$, defines a *query* on P The *answer to query* ϕ on P is the set of tuples $\{\mathbf{x} \mid K_0^P(\phi(\mathbf{x}))\}$, or, alternatively, it is defined with a *static* (time independent) predicate

$$\phi_P^*(\mathbf{x}) \;=\; K_0^P(\phi(\mathbf{x}))$$

where K^P is the temporal structure determined by program P (K_0^P means that K^P is evaluated at time $t = 0$) In other words, ϕ_P^* specifies the set of tuples $\mathbf{x}$ satisfying the temporal logic formula ϕ at time 0 with semantics determined by program P We will refer to first order logic predicate ϕ_P^* as being *induced* by temporal logic formula ϕ and program P Note that we are interested in making predictions *now* about events in the *future* For a very simple example consider ϕ $A(x)$ **atnext** $B(x)$. Then $\phi_P^*(x)$ is true at time 0 if $A(x)$ is true at the first time instance when $B(x)$ becomes true

Denote the class of all temporal logic formulae as TL and the class of all quantifier-free temporal logic formulae TL_0 Consider all the TL formulae having the form $(\exists x_1)$ $(\exists x_n)$ $\phi(x_1, \ldots, x_n)$, where $\phi(x_1, \ldots, x_n)$ is a TL_0 formula, and all the TL formulae *equivalent* to them (produce the same answers for all the temporal structures) Call this subclass of TL formulae the *existential fragment* of TL and denote it as $TL_\exists$

Given a Datalog or Datalog$^\neg$ program P, we can ask either Datalog queries or queries expressed in temporal logic on P In Section 4, we analyze the expressive powers of the two approaches, but first, we compare our work with the work of others

3 Related Work

Our work is related to research on temporal databases, work on Datalog and its extensions, and to temporal logic.

The work on temporal databases [Ar86.Sno87,Gad88,ClCr87,NaAh88,LoJo88,Tan86][7] is concerned with the issues of representing *finite* sequences of database states with the actual (materialized) data and querying these representations. In contrast, we are interested in the mechanisms that generate *infinite* sequences of database states, in general, such as Datalog and its extensions, as well as in querying the sequences generated by these mechanisms

There is a large body of research studying queries on Datalog and its extensions (we again refer the reader to [Ul188]) However, as stated before, this research does not consider temporal aspects of Datalog and is mainly interested in fixpoint queries The paper [ChIm88] constitutes an exception to this It studies evolution of databases in time by introducing a single monadic function *successor* per predicate and dividing attributes into temporal and non-temporal types. That approach to modelling time in the framework of logic programming[8] is more general than the dynamic semantics of Datalog This can be illustrated with an example a Datalog rule $A(x) \leftarrow B(x)$ can be converted to the rule $B(t,x) \rightarrow A(t+1,x)$ in the formalism of [ChIm88] In addition, the complexity of query

[7] This is list represents the scope of the work in the field and is not meant to be exhaustive

[8] Since a function symbol is introduced

processing and questions related to finiteness of least fixpoints are studied in [ChIm88]. Finally, the issues of computing infinite fixpoints with finite computations by introducing infinite objects are considered However, the semantics of programs in [ChIm88] is still defined in terms of fixpoints and is, therefore, static. In other words, queries are still asked about the predicates at the fixpoint time and not about "intermediate" stages as is done in temporal logic In contrast, we consider Datalog and Datalog¬ programs as temporal structures for temporal logic queries, and we analyze the expressive power of Datalog queries with temporal logic queries for Datalog and Datalog¬ programs

There is a large body of work on temporal logic Textbooks, such as [Kro87,ReUr71], [vBen83], provided a general description of this research However, this research considers arbitrary temporal structures, whereas we are interested in the temporal structures generated by finite formalisms such as Datalog and its extensions and in the expressive power of temporal logic queries on these structures

The paper [ClWa83] uses intentional logic [Gal75] to provide a formal semantics of historical databases It also discusses how time-related queries can be expressed in intentional logic. It is well-known that temporal logics constitute fragments of the intentional logic [Gal75] However, we use temporal logic and not the intentional logic as a query language, as it is better suited for the relational model and therefore it is more applicable to Datalog programs

As was stated before, there has been no analysis of the relative expressive powers of temporal logic and Datalog queries In the next section, we carry such an analysis In particular, we prove a surprising result that for negated Datalog with inflationary semantics, Datalog queries have the same expressive power as the domain independent (to be defined later) existential fragment of temporal logic

4 Temporal Logic vs. Datalog Queries

In this section, we compare the expressive power of temporal logic and Datalog queries for two groups of programs The first group constitutes pure Datalog programs, and the second group consists of Datalog¬ programs with the inflationary semantics (we will implicitly assume that semantics is inflationary for Datalog¬ programs in the sequel) First, we show that any Datalog query can be expressed in temporal logic with a simple formula for both types of programs

Proposition 1 *For any Datalog query Q defined on Datalog$^\neg$ program P there is a temporal logic query defined on P such that the two formulae define the same mapping*

Proof: The temporal logic formula is simply $\{\mathbf{x} \mid \diamond Q(\mathbf{x})\}$ A tuple $\mathbf{x}$ belongs to the fixpoint of P if and only if at *some* point in time $Q(\mathbf{x})$ is true. ∎

Since Datalog programs constitute a subset of Datalog$^\neg$ programs, Proposition 1 holds for Datalog programs as well

It is simple to express Datalog queries in temporal logic However, the question whether or not temporal logic queries can be expressed as Datalog queries is a non-trivial one We determine the answer to this question in the rest of this section Subsection 4 1 deals with pure Datalog and Subsection 4 2 with Datalog$^\neg$

4.1 Temporal Logic vs. Datalog Queries for Datalog

Theorem 2 *TL_0 has more expressive power than Datalog queries for Datalog programs.*

Proof: We claim that the query defined by the TL_0 formula $A(x)$ **atnext** $B(x)$ where A and B are EDBs is not expressible in Datalog The claim follows from the fact that this query is not monotone in predicate B in general In contrast, Datalog programs are monotone in all their predicates ∎

4.2 Temporal Logic vs. Datalog Queries for Negated Datalog with Inflationary Semantics

In this section, we prove the main technical result of this paper that the existential fragment TL_0 of temporal logic with mild restrictions imposed on it has the same expressive power as Datalog queries for safe negated Datalog programs with inflationary semantics Restrictions imposed on TL_0 have the following nature. The answer to a Datalog query on a safe Datalog$^\neg$ program constitutes a finite relation because safe rules cannot produce new symbols However, an arbitrary query from TL_0 can produce an infinite answer

Therefore, we define the concept of domain independence of temporal logic queries as a generalization of domain independent relational queries [Ull88] and restrict TL_0 to domain independent queries to guarantee finite answers. Formally, we will prove that for any safe Datalog$^\neg$ program P and a domain independent query ϕ on P from $TL_\exists$, there is a safe Datalog$^\neg$ program P' and a Datalog query Q such that $\phi^\bullet_P \equiv Q_{P'}$.

We also prove another stronger result: we do not restrict queries from TL_0 to be domain independent and treat infinite answers in some "uniform" fashion by introducing a special constant ω outside DOM_P such that (loosely speaking) the value of a temporal logic query on infinitely many tuples coincides with the value of the query on ω. The exact meaning of this statement will be provided later in this paper.

We structure the proof of the main result of this section as follows. First, we construct *ordering* predicates for a temporal logic query ϕ coding the order in which various tuples are added to the IDB predicates. Second, we show how these predicates can be used to produce a Datalog query "equivalent" to ϕ. Third, we show how these predicates can be produced with safe Datalog$^\neg$ programs. In the next subsection, we provide an example that illustrates these steps.

4.2.1 Example

Consider a simple temporal formula $\phi(x, y, z)$: $A(x, y)$ **atnext** $B(y, z)$. First, we define the predicates coding the order in which tuples are inserted into the IDB predicates.

Let $t_A(x, y)$ be the time instance when the tuple (x, y) is inserted into the predicate A, and let $t_B(y, z)$ be the time instance when the tuple (y, z) is inserted into the predicate B. $t_A(x, y)$ and $t_B(y, z)$ are well defined, because under the inflationary semantics of Datalog$^\neg$ once a tuple is inserted into a predicate, it will never be removed from it. In general, $0 \leq t_A(x, y), t_B(y, z) \leq \infty$. $t_A(x, y) = 0$ means that (x, y) was in A at time 0 (and therefore A was an EDB), and $t_A(x, y) = \infty$ means that (x, y) was never inserted into A, similarly for t_B.

It follows from the definition of $\phi^\bullet_P$, the predicate induced by ϕ, and from the definition of **atnext** operator that

$$\phi^\bullet_P(x, y, z) = \begin{cases} True & \text{if } t_A(x, y) \leq t_B(y, z) < \infty \\ False & \text{otherwise} \end{cases}$$

Note that by the definition of **atnext** if $t_B(y,z) = \infty$ then $\phi_P^{\bullet}(x,y,z) = False$. Furthermore, observe that the value of $\phi_P^{\bullet}(x,y,z)$ depends *only* on the relative times when $A(x,y)$ and $B(y,z)$ become true, that is when (x,y) is inserted into A and (y,z) is inserted into B.

To formally code these relative order of "insertion" times, we introduce 11 *ordering* predicates $R_{0=A=B<\infty}$, $R_{0=A<B<\infty}$, $R_{0=A<B=\infty}$, $R_{0<A=B<\infty}$, $R_{0<A<B<\infty}$, $R_{0<A<B=\infty}$, $R_{0<A=B=\infty}$, $R_{0=B<A<\infty}$, $R_{0=B<A=\infty}$, $R_{0<B<A<\infty}$, $R_{0<B<A=\infty}$. These predicates cover all possibilities of relative times of tuple insertions into predicates A and B.

The notational structure of these predicates is $R_{0\theta_0 P_1\theta_1 P_2\theta_2\infty}$, where $\theta_0, \theta_1, \theta_2 \in \{=, <\}$ and $\{P_1, P_2\} = \{A, B\}$. Such a predicate is defined by

$$R_{0\theta_0 P_1\theta_1 P_2\theta_2\infty} = \begin{cases} True & \text{if } 0\theta_0 t_{P_1}\theta_1 t_{P_2}\theta_2\infty \\ False & \text{otherwise} \end{cases}$$

For example, $R_{0<A=B<\infty}(x,y,z)$ is true if and only if (x,y) was not in A and (y,z) was not in B at time 0, and (x,y) was inserted into A and (y,z) was inserted into B at the same time instance.

Next, we show how the ordering predicates can be used to define a Datalog query equivalent to ϕ. As $\phi_P^{\bullet}(x,y,z)$ is true if and only if $t_A(x,y) \le t_B(y,z) < \infty$, it follows that $\phi_P^{\bullet}$ is equivalent to $R_{0=A=B<\infty} \vee R_{0=A<B<\infty} \vee R_{0=A<B=\infty} \vee R_{0<A=B<\infty} \vee R_{0<A<B<\infty}$[9]. Clearly, if we introduce a new predicate Q such that $Q \leftarrow R_i$ for all the five predicates R_i appearing in the previous disjunction, then Q and $\phi_P^{\bullet}$ are equivalent.

In the proof of the main theorem we will show how such ordering predicates in the disjunction can be computed with safe Datalog$^\neg$ programs. This means that ϕ is equivalent to Q on a safe Datalog$^\neg$ program.

4.2.2 Ordering Predicates for Quantifier-free Formulae

In this section, we restrict our attention only to quantifier-free temporal logic formulae TL_0.

We formally define ordering predicates on a query ϕ now. A temporal logic formula

[9] In this example it doesn't matter whether $t_A(x,y) = 0$ or $t_A(x,y) > 0$, but in general such distinctions need to be made.

can have several references to the same predicate. Each such reference will be called an *occurrence* of a predicate in a formula. Two occurrences of the same predicate are *identical* if they have the same list of variables, e.g. $P(x_1, \ldots, x_k)$, otherwise, they are *distinct*. Let $A_1, \ldots, A_n$ be all the distinct occurrences of all the predicates from query ϕ and let $(i_1, \ldots, i_n)$ be a permutation of $(1, \ldots, n)$.

For example, the formula $B(x)$ **atnext** $(B(y) \wedge C(x,x))$ gives 3 predicates, which we could write as $A_1(x)$, $A_2(y)$, $A_3(x,x)$.

Let $\mathbf{x}$ be a sequence of some length m listing in some order all the variables of ϕ. For each predicate A_i, $\mathbf{x}_i$ will denote the actual variables of A_i in the order they appear. Thus in the above example, $m = 2$, $\mathbf{x} = (x,y)$, $\mathbf{x}_1 = (x)$, $\mathbf{x}_2 = (y)$, $\mathbf{x}_3 = (x,x)$. As defined in Section 4.2.1, $t_{A_i}(\mathbf{x}_i)$ will denote the time instance when $\mathbf{x}_i$ is inserted into A_i. As before, $t_{A_i}(\mathbf{x}_i) = \infty$ means that $\mathbf{x}_i$ is not inserted into A_i at all.

For *each* permutation $(i_1, i_2, \ldots, i_n)$ of $(1, 2, \ldots, n)$, we define a set of *ordering* predicates $R_{0\theta_{i_0}A_{i_1}\theta_{i_1}A_{i_2}\theta_{i_2}\ldots A_{i_n}\theta_{i_n}\infty}(\mathbf{x})$, where $\theta_{i_0}, \theta_{i_1}, \ldots, \theta_{i_n}$ vary over $\{=, <\}$, and at least one of them is $<$. Generalizing from Section 4.2.1, $R_{0\theta_{i_0}A_{i_1}\theta_{i_1}A_{i_2}\theta_{i_2}\ldots A_{i_n}\theta_{i_n}\infty}(\mathbf{x})$ is true if and only if $0\theta_{i_0}t_{A_{i_1}}(\mathbf{x}_{i_1})\theta_{i_1}t_{A_{i_2}}(\mathbf{x}_{i_2})\theta_{i_2}\ldots t_{A_{i_n}}(\mathbf{x}_{i_n})\theta_{i_n}\infty$.

To avoid cumbersome notation we denote the set of *all* the ordering predicates by $R = \{R_i | i \in I\}$ for an appropriate index set I.

Next, we state a technical lemma needed to prove Lemma 4.

Lemma 3 *Let* $\alpha(\mathbf{x}) = 0\theta_{i_0}t_{A_{i_1}}(\mathbf{x}_{i_1})\theta_{i_1}t_{A_{i_2}}(\mathbf{x}_{i_2})\theta_{i_2}\ldots t_{A_{i_n}}(\mathbf{x}_{i_n})\theta_{i_n}\infty$.

Define the intervals of natural numbers, $I_0, I_1, \ldots, I_n$ *by*

$$I_j(\mathbf{x}) = \begin{cases} [0, t_{A_{i_1}}(\mathbf{x}_{i_1})) & \text{if } j = 0, \\ [t_{A_{i_j}}(\mathbf{x}_{i_j}), t_{A_{i_{j+1}}}(\mathbf{x}_{i_{j+1}})) & \text{if } j = 1, 2, \ldots, n-1, \\ [t_{A_{i_n}}(\mathbf{x}_{i_n}), \infty) & \text{if } j = n \end{cases}$$

Let $T(\phi(\mathbf{x}))$ *be the set of time instances in which* $\phi(\mathbf{x})$ *is true. Then there is a subset of indices* $j_1, j_2, \ldots, j_k$ *such that* $T(\phi(\mathbf{x}))$ *is the union of non-empty intervals* $I_{j_1}(\mathbf{x}) \ldots I_{j_k}(\mathbf{x})$ *for all* $\mathbf{x}$ *satisfying* $\alpha(\mathbf{x})$. *This means that the indices* $j_1, \ldots, j_k$ *do not depend on* $\mathbf{x}$.

Proof: Without loss of generality, assume that $i_j = j$ for each j, and define $t_0 = 0$, $t_{n+1} = \infty$. Note that some of the intervals may be empty and they are all disjoint. We prove the lemma by induction on the number of operators in ϕ, which without loss of generality are $\neg, \vee$, **atnext** Recall that we *only* consider $\mathbf{x}$ satisfying $\alpha(\mathbf{x})$.

1 ϕ is A_i for some i Then $T(\phi(\mathbf{x})) = \cup\{I_j(\mathbf{x}) | j \geq i \wedge I_j(\mathbf{x}) \neq \emptyset\}$ The choice of intervals clearly does not depend on $\mathbf{x}$ (as long as $\alpha(\mathbf{x})$)

2 ϕ is $\neg\phi_1$ By induction, $T(\phi_1(\mathbf{x})) = \cup\{I_j(\mathbf{x}) | j \in J_1\}$, where J_1 does not depend on $\mathbf{x}$. Then $T(\phi(\mathbf{x})) = \cup\{I_j(\mathbf{x}) | j \notin J_1 \wedge I_j(\mathbf{x}) \neq \emptyset\}$ Note that the set of intervals does not depend on $\mathbf{x}$

3 ϕ is $\phi_1 \vee \phi_2$ By induction, $T(\phi_1(\mathbf{x})) = \cup\{I_j(\mathbf{x}) | j \in J_1\}$ and $T(\phi_2(\mathbf{x})) = \cup\{I_j(\mathbf{x}) | j \in J_2\}$, where J_1, J_2 do not depend on $\mathbf{x}$ Then $T(\phi(\mathbf{x})) = \cup\{I_j(\mathbf{x}) | j \in J_1 \cup J_2\}$ Clearly, the set of intervals over which $T(\phi(\mathbf{x}))$ is true does not depend on $\mathbf{x}$

4 ϕ is (ϕ_1 **atnext** ϕ_2) Let $J'(j) = \{j' | (j' \geq j) \wedge (I_{j'}(\mathbf{x}) \neq \emptyset) \wedge (I_{j'}(\mathbf{x}) \subseteq T(\phi_2(\mathbf{x})))\}$ and let

$$\mu(j) = \begin{cases} \min(J'(j)) & \text{if } J'(j) \neq \emptyset \\ n+1 & \text{otherwise} \end{cases}$$

Both μ and J' are well-defined because, by induction, the set of intervals comprising $T(\phi_2(\mathbf{x}))$ does not depend on $\mathbf{x}$ and because whether or not $I_{j'}(\mathbf{x}) \neq \emptyset$ also does not depend on $\mathbf{x}$

Then,

$T(\phi(\mathbf{x})) = \cup\{I_j | (I_{\mu(j)} \subseteq T(\phi_1(\mathbf{x}))) \wedge (\mu(j) \leq n)\}$

By induction, the choice of intervals in ϕ_1 does not depend on $\mathbf{x}$ Therefore, the set of intervals comprising $T(\phi(\mathbf{x}))$ also does not depend on $\mathbf{x}$

∎

Lemma 4 *Let ϕ be a TL_0 formula. Then for each i either* $(\forall\mathbf{x})(R_i(\mathbf{x}) \Rightarrow \phi_P^* (\mathbf{x}))$ *or* $(\forall\mathbf{x})(R_i(\mathbf{x}) \Rightarrow \neg\, \phi_P^* (\mathbf{x}))$

Proof. Since $R_i(\mathbf{x})$ holds if and only if the corresponding $\alpha_i(\mathbf{x})$ holds, based on Lemma 3, all we have to do is to check if $I_0(\mathbf{x}) \subseteq T(\phi_0(\mathbf{x}))$ ∎

The above lemma partitions the index set I into two subsets I_{True} and I_{False} where $I_{True} = \{i \mid (\forall \mathbf{x})(R_i(\mathbf{x}) \Rightarrow \phi_P^* (\mathbf{x}))\}$ and $I_{False} = \{i \mid (\forall \mathbf{x})(R_i(\mathbf{x}) \Rightarrow \neg \phi_P^* (\mathbf{x}))\}$. The next lemma says that the answer to a query from TL_0 is determined by some set of ordering predicates

Lemma 5 *For any TL_0 formula ϕ and for all* $\mathbf{x}$, $\bigvee_{i \in I_{True}} R_i(\mathbf{x}) = \phi_P^*(\mathbf{x})$

Proof: One part of the lemma follows from Lemma 4 To prove the other part, consider any value of $\mathbf{x}$ Since R_i's are collectively exhaustive, $R_i(\mathbf{x})$ will be true for some $i \in I$ In addition, it is easy to see that this i is in I_{True} ∎

Note that the set I_{True} is defined *only* by the formula ϕ and is independent of the program P or the values of the EDBs

Based on the above, the computation of ϕ_P^* can be reduced to the computation of the individual predicates R_i We will examine under which conditions they can be computed with safe Datalog$^\neg$ programs

We define the set of *base ordering* predicates for the predicate instances $A_1, A_2, \ldots, A_n$ from ϕ. For any $i, j = 1, 2, \ldots, n$, let $\mathbf{x}_{i,j}$ denote some sequence listing the union of the variables in $\mathbf{x}_i$ and $\mathbf{x}_j$ Then the base ordering predicates are divided into four types, each of them being defined as follows

1 $S_{0=A_i}(\mathbf{x}_i)$ for $i = 1, 2, \ldots, n$ $S_{0=A_i}(\mathbf{x}_i)$ is true if and only if $0 = t_{A_i}(\mathbf{x}_i)$

2 $S_{0<A_i=A_j<\infty}(\mathbf{x}_{i,j})$ for $i, j = 1, 2, \ldots, n$. $S_{0<A_i=A_j<\infty}(\mathbf{x}_{i,j})$ is true if and only if $0 < t_{A_i}(\mathbf{x}_i) = t_{A_j}(\mathbf{x}_j) < \infty$

3 $S_{0<A_i<A_j<\infty}(\mathbf{x}_{i,j})$ for $i, j = 1, 2, \ldots, n$ $S_{0<A_i<A_j<\infty}(\mathbf{x}_{i,j})$ is true if and only if $0 < t_{A_i}(\mathbf{x}_i) < t_{A_j}(\mathbf{x}_j) < \infty$

4 $S_{A_i=\infty}(\mathbf{x}_i)$ for $i = 1, 2, \ldots, n$ $S_{A_i=\infty}(\mathbf{x}_i)$ is true if and only if $t_{A_i}(\mathbf{x}_i) = \infty$

Predicates of types 1, 2, and 3 will be called *bounded*, predicate of type 4 will be called *unbounded*

Note that, for example, $R_{0=A_4<A_3=A_1<A_2=A_5=\infty} \equiv S_{0=A_4} \wedge S_{0<A_3=A_1<\infty} \wedge S_{A_2=\infty} \wedge S_{A_5=\infty}$ Generally,

Lemma 6 *Let $\{S_j | j \in J\}$ be some enumeration of the base ordering predicates Each ordering predicate R_i is equivalent to $\bigwedge_{j \in J_i} S_j$ for some $J_i \subseteq J$*

Proof: Follows from the fact that any $0\theta_{i_0} A_{i_1} \theta_{i_1} A_{i_2} \theta_{i_2} \ldots A_{i_n} \theta_{i_n} \infty$ can be represented as a conjunction of a set of formulae of the form $0 = A_i$, $0 < A_i = A_j < \infty$, $0 < A_i < A_j < \infty$, $A_i = \infty$ ∎

Lemma 7 *Bounded base ordering predicates can be computed by safe Datalog$^{\neg}$ rules*

Proof: We consider each of the three types in turn and show for each type how to compute predicates of this type with safe rules

1. $S_{0=A_i}(\mathbf{x}_i)$ can be true only if A_i is an EDB and $A_i(\mathbf{x}_i)$ holds For each EDB A_i we write the rule. $S_{0=A_i}(\mathbf{x}_i) \leftarrow A_i(\mathbf{x}_i)$. No rules are written for IDBs

2. To handle this type we want to state that there is a (finite) instance in time $t > 0$ such that $A_i(\mathbf{x}_i)$ and $A_j(\mathbf{x}_j)$ both become true for the first time (simultaneously) Thus, we want to say that for some t, $A_i(\mathbf{x}_i)$ and $A_j(\mathbf{x}_j)$ were false at time $t-1$ and became true at time t To handle this, for each IDB A_i, we introduce a *trailing* predicate A'_i with the property that if $A_i(\mathbf{x}_i)$ became true at t, $A'_i(\mathbf{x}_i)$ becomes true at time $t+1$ Such IDBs A'_i can be computed by the rules $A'_i(\mathbf{x}_i) \leftarrow A_i(\mathbf{x}_i)$ Using the trailing predicates, we write the rules $S_{0<A_i=A_j<\infty}(\mathbf{x}_{i,j}) \leftarrow A_i(\mathbf{x}_i) \wedge \neg A'_i(\mathbf{x}_i) \wedge A_j(\mathbf{x}_j) \wedge A'_j(\mathbf{x}_j)$

3. To handle this type, we use the trailing predicates defined above and the rules computing them The derivation is slightly non-intuitive, but the predicates can be computed after adding the rules $S_{0<A_i<A_j<\infty}(\mathbf{x}_{i,j}) \leftarrow A'_i(\mathbf{x}_i) \wedge A_j(\mathbf{x}_j) \wedge \neg A'_j(\mathbf{x}_j)$

∎

Note that the unbounded predicates cannot in general be computed with safe Datalog$^{\neg}$ programs because they are in general infinite, as is the case for the formula $\neg(\neg A(x)$ atnext $A(x))$ which is true for all x and for all programs We will provide two solutions to this problem The first solution is to restrict the consideration of TL_0 formulae to the class of *domain independent* formulae, to be defined below, that guarantee finite instances of unbounded predicates The second approach will be discussed in Section 4 2 4 To define domain independence, we introduce first the notion of the domain of a temporal logic query with respect to a program

Definition 8 *Given a Datalog$^\neg$ program P and a temporal logic formula ϕ, the domain of ϕ with respect to P, $dom_{P,\phi}$, is the set of all the constants appearing in ϕ, the constants appearing in all the EDB predicates of P, in rules of P, and the constants in all the future instances of predicates in P, i e constants inferred by program P*

Since we consider only *safe* programs, no new constants will be added to $dom_{P,\phi}$ by applying rules from P Therefore, the domain of a safe formula contains only constants in ϕ, in EDB predicates, and the remaining constants of P The domain of ϕ with respect to P, $dom_{P,\phi}$, gives rise to a predicate on DOM_P which is true on the elements of $dom_{P,\phi}$ and only on these elements. If no confusion arises, we will use the same notation for that predicate as for the domain itself Also, $dom_{P,\phi}(x_1, \ldots, x_n)$ will denote $dom_{P,\phi}(x_1) \wedge \ldots \wedge dom_{P,\phi}(x_n)$

Using Definition 8, *domain independence* is defined as follows

Definition 9 *A temporal logic formula ϕ is domain independent if for any safe Datalog$^\neg$ program P the predicate ϕ^*_P is the same for any domain $DOM_P \supseteq dom_{P,\phi}$, i e ϕ^*_P does not depend on DOM_P.*

Note that Definition 9 constitutes an extension of the definition of a domain independent formula [Ull88] to temporal logic and Datalog$^\neg$ programs Also note that a domain independent query returns only finite answers, each constant in the answer contained in the domain $dom_{P,\phi}$ Using the notions just defined, we can state the following lemma

Lemma 10 *For each base ordering predicate $S_{A_i=\infty}$, the predicate $S'_{A_i=\infty} \cdot S_{A_i=\infty} \wedge dom_{P,\phi}$ can be computed with safe Datalog$^\neg$ rules*

Proof: The key observation is that a safe Datalog$^\neg$ program reaches a fixpoint and it is possible to detect this fixpoint using safe Datalog$^\neg$ rules, since $dom_{P,\phi}$ is finite

Let FP be the *flag predicate*, which becomes true one time instance after the fixpoint is reached Then

$$S'_{A_i=\infty}(\mathbf{x}_i) \leftarrow FP \wedge dom_{P,\phi}(\mathbf{x}) \wedge \neg A_i(\mathbf{x}_i)$$

Clearly, the *predicate* $dom_{P,\phi}$ can be computed with a Datalog program

To finish the proof, note that FP can be computed using the rule

$$FP \leftarrow \wedge_{i=1}^{n}((\forall \mathbf{x}_i)(A_i(\mathbf{x}_i) \Rightarrow A_i'(\mathbf{x}_i)))$$

The rule says that FP becomes true when the predicates in P stop changing over time i e. at the fixpoint time This rule is not normalized, however, the variables $\mathbf{x}_i$ range over the domain $dom_{P,\phi}$, which is finite Therefore, we can remove universal quantifiers and replace them with finite conjunctions After that, the rule can be normalized to a set of safe Datalog$^\neg$ rules ∎

4.2.3 Main Theorem for the Domain-independent Case

In Section 4.2 2, we defined ordering and base ordering predicates and showed how ordering predicates can be used to compute the answer to a query We also showed how base ordering predicates could be computed with safe Datalog$^\neg$ rules We are ready to put these results together now and to state the preliminary version of the main theorem in the following lemma

Lemma 11 *For any safe Datalog$^\neg$ program P over some (possibly infinite) domain DOM_P and any domain independent temporal logic query ϕ in TL_0, there exists a safe Datalog$^\neg$ program P' over DOM_P and a Datalog query Q, such that ϕ_P^* and $Q_{P'}$ define the same predicate, where $Q_{P'}$ denotes the IDB Q as computed by program P'*

Proof: Based on Lemmas 5 and 6, we can write

$$\phi_P^* \equiv \vee_{i\in I_{True}} \wedge_{j\in J_i} S_j \tag{1}$$

Observe that for base ordering predicates of of type 1, 2, and 3 $S_j \equiv S_j \wedge dom_{P,\phi}$, and to simplify subsequent discussion we will write S_j' for S_j for predicates of this type (For base ordering predicates of type 4, S_j' was introduced already in the proof of Lemma 10)

Since ϕ_P^* is domain independent,

$$\phi_P^* \equiv \phi_P^* \wedge dom_{P,\phi} \equiv \vee_{i\in I_{True}} \wedge_{j\in J_i} (S_j \wedge dom_{P,\phi})$$

which can be also written as

$$\phi_P^* \equiv \vee_{i \in I_{True}} \wedge_{j \in J_i} S_j' \tag{2}$$

From Lemmas 7 and 10 we know that all S_j', $j \in J$ can be computed with safe Datalog$^\neg$ rules

The program P' consists of program P, the programs that compute predicates S_j' for $j \in J$ and the following set of rules

$Q(\mathbf{x}) \leftarrow R_i(\mathbf{x})$, for $i \in I_{True}$

$R_i(\mathbf{x}) \leftarrow \wedge_{j \in J_i} S_j'(\mathbf{x}_j')$, for $i \in I_{True}$

where $\mathbf{x}_j'$ denotes the variables of S_j', and Q is an IDB predicate not appearing in other rules Q constitutes the query in question It follows from (2) that Q and ϕ_P^* define the same predicate ∎

Now, we are ready to state the main theorem in the version for domain independent formulae

Theorem 12 *For any safe Datalog$^\neg$ program P over some domain DOM_P and any domain independent temporal logic query ϕ in $TL_\exists$, there exists a safe Datalog$^\neg$ program P' over DOM_P and a Datalog query Q such that ϕ_P^* and $Q_{P'}$ define the same predicate.*

Proof: Consider a $TL_\exists$ formula ϕ By the definition of $TL_\exists$, ϕ can be written as $(\exists \mathbf{x})\phi'(\mathbf{x})$ where ϕ' is quantifier-free By the previous lemma, we can find a program and a query Q' that computes the same result as ϕ' Take projection of Q' on the free variables of ϕ to obtain the result. ∎

Corollary 13 *Let P be a safe Datalog$^\neg$ program over some domain DOM_P and let ϕ from $TL_\exists$ be such that all the base ordering predicates appearing in ϕ_P^* as described in (1) are bounded Then there exists a safe Datalog$^\neg$ program P' over DOM_P whose rules do not contain constants from the EDBs in P and a Datalog query Q, such that ϕ_P^* and $Q_{P'}$ define the same predicate*

Proof: Note that we dropped the domain independence requirement because it appeared only in connection with unbounded predicates The proof follows immediately from the construction of the rules computing the bounded base ordering predicates ∎

Example 1

We return to the example at the beginning of the introduction The program P was

```
cousin(X,Y) :- parent(X,Xp) & parent(Y,Yp) & parent(XP,Z) & parent(YP,Z)
          & XP ≠ YP

cousin(X,Y)  - parent(X,Xp) & parent(Y,Yp) & cousin(Xp,Yp).
```

We were interested in computing relation *closerCousin*(x, y, u, v) defined with the temporal logic formula *cousin*(x, y) **before** *cousin*(u, v) The following Datalog$^{\neg}$ program computes *closerCousins* in a way outlined in the proof of Theorem 12

```
cousin(X,Y) ·- parent(X,Xp) & parent(Y,Yp) & parent(XP,Z) & parent(YP,Z)
          & XP ≠ YP

cousin(X,Y)  - parent(X,Xp) & parent(Y,Yp) & cousin(Xp,Yp)

cousin'(X,Y)   - cousin(X,Y)

closerCousins(X,Y,U,V)  .- cousin'(X,Y) & cousin(U,V) & ¬cousin'(U,V)
```

Another interesting example constitutes the program computing *closerThen* relationship based on transitive closure relationship *transClosure*. *closerThan*(x, y, u, v) is defined as *transClosure*(x, y) **before** *transClosure*(u, v) As before, a Datalog¬ program can be used to compute *closerThan*, thus computing which pairs of nodes in the graph are closer to each other than other pairs of nodes

∎

Corollary 14 *For any domain independent query ϕ from $TL_{\exists}$ and a safe Datalog$^{\neg}$ program P there is a predicate Q and a safe Datalog$^{\neg}$ program P' such that $\phi^{*}_{P}(\mathbf{x}) = K_0^{P'}(\diamond Q(\mathbf{x}))$, where (as was defined in Section 2) $K_0^{P'}$ is a temporal structure defined by program P' taken at present time.*

Proof: Follows from Theorem 12 and Proposition 1 ∎

This corollary proves the collapse of the domain independent existential fragment of temporal logic but *only* for temporal structures determined by Datalog$^{\neg}$ programs with inflationary semantics Specifically, any domain independent $TL_{\exists}$ formula can be reduced to a simple formula $\diamond Q$ (but for a different program)

The next proposition says, among other things, that not all the temporal logic queries can be obtained with Datalog queries over safe Datalog$^{\neg}$ programs. Therefore, temporal logic queries have, generally, more expressive power than Datalog queries over safe Datalog$^{\neg}$ programs with inflationary semantics.

Proposition 15 *For any domain dependent query ϕ and a safe program P there is no safe program P' and a query Q such that Q and ϕ^{*}_{P} define the same mapping.*

Proof: Follows from the fact that safe Datalog$^{\neg}$ programs can produce only symbols in $dom_{P,\phi}$, whereas domain independent queries return elements outside of this domain. ∎

4.2.4 Main Theorem for the Domain Dependent Case

We now show how to answer queries in $TL_{\exists}$ that are not domain-independent. Strictly speaking, this cannot be done using safe Datalog$^{\neg}$ programs, as those programs can only compute finite predicates, whereas answers to domain-dependent queries, can in general, be infinite. However, we can provide a simple metaprocedure to do so using safe Datalog$^{\neg}$ programs.

Let ϕ be an arbitrary query in $TL_{\exists}$. Let ω be a constant not in DOM_P, and let Ω be a unary predicate not in P. Let $DOM_{P'} = DOM_P \cup \{\omega\}$. Add a new fact $\Omega(\omega)$ to P, obtaining P'. The purpose of this rule is to enlarge the domain of the original program, allowing the utilization of the new constant ω. Note that $dom_{P',\phi} = dom_{P,\phi} \cup \{\omega\}$. As in the proof of Lemma 11, we can compute $\phi^{*}_{P'} \wedge dom_{P',\phi}$ using safe Datalog$^{\neg}$ rules.

Let $\mathbf{x} = (x_1, x_2, \ldots, x_m)$, where x_i, $i = 1, 2, \ldots, m$ range over the whole domain DOM_P and define $\mathbf{x}[\omega]$ as $(x'_1, x'_2, \ldots, x'_m)$, where for each i, $x'_i = x_i$ if $x_i \in dom_{P',\phi}$, and $x'_i = \omega$ if $x_i \notin dom_{P',\phi}$.

Clearly, for all $\mathbf{x} \in DOM_P^{|\mathbf{x}|}$, $\phi^{*}_{P}(\mathbf{x}) = \phi^{*}_{P'}(\mathbf{x})$. However, one can also show that for each $\mathbf{x}$, $\phi^{*}_{P'}(\mathbf{x})$ is true if and only if $\phi^{*}_{P'}(\mathbf{x}[\omega])$ is true. In other words, if some component x_i of $\mathbf{x}$ lies outside $dom_{P,\phi}$, *it does not matter* for the truth-value of $\phi^{*}_{P'}$ what the actual value of x_i is (as long as it is outside $dom_{P,\phi}$). Therefore, to determine whether $\phi^{*}_{P'}(\mathbf{x})$ is true, it is enough to determine whether $\phi^{*}_{P'}(\mathbf{x}[\omega])$ is true. But $\mathbf{x}[\omega]$ ranges over $dom_{P',\phi}^{|\mathbf{x}|}$. Therefore, it is enough to compute $\phi^{*}_{P'}(\mathbf{x})$ on $dom_{P',\phi}^{|\mathbf{x}|}$. It follows from Lemma 11 that $\phi^{*}_{P'}(\mathbf{x}) \wedge dom_{P',\phi}^{|\mathbf{x}|}$ is computable with safe Datalog$^{\neg}$ rules. Therefore, we proved the following theorem.

Theorem 16 *For any safe Datalog$^{\neg}$ program P over some domain DOM_P and any temporal logic query ϕ in $TL_{\exists}$, there exists a safe Datalog$^{\neg}$ program P'' over $DOM_P \cup \{\omega\}$ where $\omega \notin DOM_P$ and a Datalog query Q such that for any $\mathbf{x}$ over DOM_P $\phi_P^{*}(\mathbf{x})$ if and only if $Q_{P''}(\mathbf{x}[\omega])$.*

Note that the replacement of $\mathbf{x}$ by $\mathbf{x}[\omega]$ cannot be done by safe Datalog$^{\neg}$ rules and, therefore, we partially "step outside of" our formalism.

5 Conclusions

In this paper, we proposed a query language for dynamic databases The syntax of this language is based on the future-related fragment of temporal logic and its semantics on Datalog programs or their extensions (e.g Datalog$^{\neg}$ with inflationary semantics) We compared this language with ordinary Datalog queries in terms of expressive power It was shown that temporal logic has strictly more expressive power than Datalog queries for Datalog and Datalog$^{\neg}$ programs with inflationary semantics However, for Datalog$^{\neg}$ programs with inflationary semantics we have proven the surprising result that the domain independent existential fragment of temporal logic has the same expressive power as Datalog queries[10] This result implies the collapse of the domain independent existential fragment of temporal logic for Datalog$^{\neg}$ programs with inflationary semantics

Temporal logic as a query language has some other important advantages over Datalog queries besides more expressive power. First, it is more general than Datalog queries because temporal logic can be asked on programs that have no fixpoints, whereas Datalog queries depend on the existence of a canonical fixpoint, and because it can be used with other formalisms besides Datalog In other words, temporal logic can be used in the contexts where Datalog queries have no meaning Second, as we have argued, temporal logic is generally easier to use than Datalog queries in the cases when temporal logic queries can be expressed with Datalog queries some temporal logic queries can be expressed only in a very complicated way in Datalog

There has been substantial research conducted recently on integrating production systems with databases The special issue of the SIGMOD Record [SIGMOD89] provides

[10]Some of our results can be generalized to formulae outside the existential fragment

an overview of this work Also, [AbVi89] studied an extension of Datalog¬ with negations allowed both in the head and in the body of a rule. Clearly, these two formalisms are isomorphic In both of these approaches, Datalog queries do not make sense in general because a fixpoint of a program may not exist However, temporal logic queries on these extensions are well-defined, and, we believe, more natural In [KeTu89], we proposed a general approach to defining dynamic databases based on Relational Discrete Event Systems and Models (RDESes and RDEMs). All the formalisms mentioned in this paper constitute examples of RDEMs. It turns out that *any* RDEM, and not only Datalog and Datalog¬, can be used as a semantic basis for temporal logic queries This makes temporal logic a powerful approach for defining queries on dynamic databases

Acknowledgements

We would like to thank Haim Gaifman, Yuri Gurevich, and Mihalis Yannakakis for useful discussions Corollary 14 was suggested to us by Haim Gaifman

References

[SIGMOD89] SIGMOD Record September 1989 Special issue on rule management and processing in expert database systems

[AbVi88] S Abiteboul and V. Vianu Procedural and declarative database update languages In *Proceedings of PODS Symposium*, pages 240–250, 1988

[AbVi89] S Abiteboul and V Vianu Fixpoint extensions of first-order logic and Datalog-like languages In *IEEE Symposium on Logic in Computer Science*, 1989

[AbVi90] S Abiteboul and V Vianu A transaction-based approach to relational database specification. *to appear in JACM* (Technical Report CS87-102, University of California at San Diego, August 1987)

[Ar86] G Ariav A temporally oriented data model *TODS*, 11(4) 499–527, 1986

[ChIm88] J Chomicki and T Imielinski Temporal deductive databases and infinite objects In *Proceedings of PODS Symposium*, pages 61–73, 1988

[ClCr87] J Clifford and A Croker The historical data model (HRDM) and algebra based on lifespans In *Proceedings of the International Conference on Data Engineering*, 1987 IEEE Computer Society

[ClWa83] J Clifford and D. S. Warren Formal semantics for time in databases *TODS*, 8(2) 214–254, 1983

[Gad88] S K Gadia A homogeneous relational model and query languages for temporal databases *TODS*, 13(4).418–448, 1988.

[Gal75] D Gallin. *Intensional and Higher-Order Modal Logic* North-Holland, Amsterdam, 1975

[GiTa86] S. Ginsburg and K Tanaka Computation-tuple sequences and object histories *ACM Transactions on Database Systems* 11(2) 186–212 1986

[GuSh86] Y Gurevich and S Shelah Fixed-point extensions of first-order logic *Annals of Pure and Applied Logic*, 32 265–280, 1986

[KeTu89] Z M Kedem and A S Tuzhilin. Relational database behavior utilizing relational discrete event systems and models. In *Proceedings of the ACM Symposium on Principles of Database Systems*, 1989

[KoPa88] P G. Kolaitis and C H Papadimitriou Why not negation by fixpoint? In *Proceedings of PODS Symposium*, pages 231–239, 1988

[Kro87] F. Kroger *Temporal Logic of Programs* Springer-Verlag, 1987 EATCS Monographs on Theoretical Computer Science.

[LoJo88] N A. Lorentzos and R. G Johnson TRA a model for a temporal relational algebra In C. Rolland, F Bodart, and M Leonard, editors, *Temporal Aspects in Information Systems*, pages 95–108, North-Holland, 1988

[McArt76] R P McArthur *Tense Logic* D Reidel Publishing Company, 1976

[NaAh88] S B. Navathe and R Ahmed. TSQL – a language interface for history databases In C Rolland, F Bodart, and M Leonard, editors, *Temporal Aspects in Information Systems*, pages 109–122, North-Holland, 1988

[ReUr71] N Rescher and A Urquhart *Temporal Logic* Springer-Verlag, 1971

[SeSh87] A Segev and A. Shoshani Logical modeling of temporal data In *Proceedings of ACM SIGMOD Conference*, pages 454–466, 1987

[Sno87] R Snodgrass. The temporal query language TQuel *TODS*, 12(2) 247–298, 1987

[Tan86] A U Tansel Adding time dimension to relational model and extending relational algebra *Information Systems*, 11 343–355, 1986

[Ull88] J Ullman *Principles of Database and Knowledge-Base Systems* Volume 1 Computer Science Press, 1988 [vBen83] J van Benthem *The Logic of Time* D Reidel Publishing Company, 1983

[Via87] V Vianu. Dynamic functional dependencies and database aging *JACM*, 34(1) 28–59, 1987

www.ingramcontent.com/pod-product-compliance
Lightning Source LLC
LaVergne TN
LVHW011941060326
832903LV00045B/39
* 9 7 8 1 0 1 9 4 2 0 0 2 7 *